© 1990 Franklin Watts

Franklin Watts Inc
387 Park Avenue South
New York, NY 10016

Printed in Belgium

Designed by
K and Co

Photographs by
NASA
TASS
ESA
Aerospatiale
British Aerospace (Space Systems)
CEF, Bernard (Paris)
Centre Optique du CSG/CNES
Lockheed Missiles and Space Company
Orbital Sciences Corporation
Armagh Planetarium

Technical Consultants
L. J. Carter
S. Young

Library of Congress Cataloging-in-Publication Data

Barrett, Norman S
The picture world of rockets and satellites / Norman Barrett.
        p.   cm. — (Picture world)
    Summary: Looks at the various uses for artificial satellites,
explaining how they orbit the earth, and how rockets are used to put
them into space.
    ISBN 0-531-14055-5
    1. Rockets (Aeronautics)—Juvenile literature. 2. Artificial
satellites—Juvenile literature. [1. Rockets (Aeronautics)
2. Artificial satellites.] I. Title. II. Series.
TL782.5.S74 1990
629.46—dc20
                                                              90-12020
                                                              CIP   AC

The Picture World of

Rockets
AND
Satellites

119281

N. S. Barrett

CONTENTS

Franklin Watts

New York • London • Sydney • Toronto

Introduction

Hundreds of satellites circle the Earth high up in space. They all have a job to do. Some carry TV, radio and telephone signals. Some produce maps of the Earth or help weather forecasters. Others are used by scientists.

Powerful rockets are needed to put satellites into space. Rockets are also used to launch manned spacecraft or send out probes to study the planets.

△ A satellite in orbit. The orbit is the path it takes around the Earth or any other body. Satellites can be any shape, because there is no air in space to cause drag.

▷ A rocket on the launch pad, about to take a satellite into orbit. Rockets are streamlined, with a cone-shaped nose, because they have to fly through the Earth's dense atmosphere.

▽ A satellite being launched from the cargo bay of a space shuttle. Shuttles are rocketed into orbit. Once there, they may place satellites in orbit or rocket them to higher orbits.

How rockets work

Rockets work by burning fuel to make gases. These rush out of the bottom of the rocket, sending it off at great speed in the other direction. This is like untying the neck of a balloon and letting it go – the escaping air sends it flying off.

A nozzle, or opening, at the bottom of the rocket is designed to allow the gases to escape smoothly. It also helps to control the rocket's direction.

▷ Hot gases shoot out of the bottom of a rocket, speeding it off the launch pad. Most rockets have separate stages. As each stage uses up its fuel, it drops away. The top stage releases the satellite or spacecraft.

▽ An illustration showing how the *Apollo* spacecraft separated from the last stage (left) of its rocket on the way to landing men on the Moon.

9

Rocket power

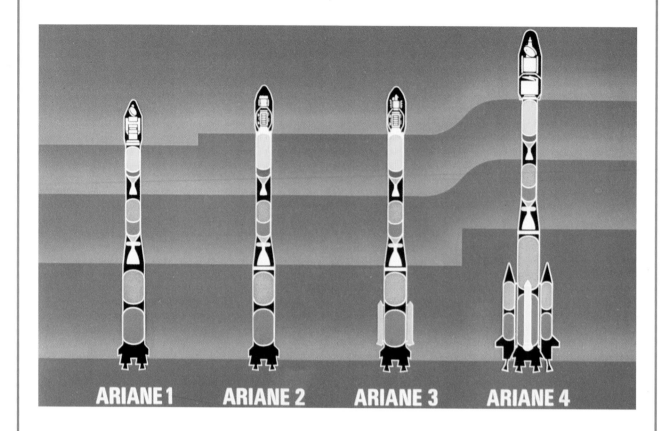

ARIANE 1   ARIANE 2   ARIANE 3   ARIANE 4

The greater the weight of a rocket and its payload, the more power is needed to launch it into space. With multistage rockets, the weight gets lighter as each stage drops off.

Rockets use enormous amounts of propellant. This consists of a fuel and a substance that supplies oxygen which is needed for the fuel to burn. It also enables the rocket to work in space, where there is no air.

△ Versions 1 to 4 of the European rocket Ariane. Ariane 4, the latest and most powerful version, can launch payloads of over four tons.
▷ An American Titan 2 rocket launches a *Gemini* spacecraft on a test flight in 1965. Special photography shows a section of the launch tower folding down as the rocket moves off.

◁ A mechanic works on the third-stage engine of an Ariane rocket. The main part of a rocket engine is the combustion chamber, where the fuel burns. It also has pumps driven by their own turbine engine.

▽ A Soviet Energia rocket with the space shuttle *Buran*. Energia, the world's most powerful rocket, can lift a payload of 100 tons into space.

∇ A *Mercury* spacecraft is launched on an Atlas rocket in the early days of unmanned American spaceflight.

△ The *Voyager 1* space probe is launched on a Titan-Centaur rocket in 1977 to begin its journey to the giant planets and beyond.

13

Space shuttles are spacecraft that can be reused. They are launched like rockets. The U.S. shuttle has two rocket boosters, which fall away when their fuel is spent.

The shuttle has its own rocket engines, which are fed by a huge external fuel tank. This is also jettisoned when the fuel is used up.

The rocket boosters fall to Earth on parachutes and are reusable. The fuel tank burns up in the atmosphere.

△ A Soviet A-2 rocket, capable of lifting 7.5 tons into orbit, launches a *Soyuz* spacecraft towards the *Mir* space station in 1988 from the Baikonur Cosmodrome spaceport.

▷ The U.S. space shuttle *Columbia* is dwarfed by the external fuel tank and the two booster rockets. The shuttle engines can be seen under the tail fin.

Kinds of satellites

Satellites are used for many different purposes. They can be any shape, and their size and weight are limited only by the lifting power of the rocket launching them.

They send information back to Earth as radio signals. These are transformed into words, figures, pictures or sounds.

▽ The Long Duration Exposure Facility (LDEF) was launched in 1984 to study the long-term effects of space on various materials. It contained 57 scientific experiments, and was retrieved by the shuttle *Columbia* in 1990.

△ *Meteosat* is a weather satellite. It sends back pictures of Earth and its cloud cover at regular intervals. This helps forecasters to predict the weather.

▷ A mapping satellite is equipped not only for mapping the Earth's surface, but also to provide information for such purposes as checking soil conditions and tracing ocean currents.

◁ A communications satellite, *Olympus 1*. The wing-like solar arrays on satellites use the Sun to produce electric power to keep the satellite working. *Olympus 1* provides several services, including direct broadcast TV.

▽ Some satellites are sent up to orbit other planets. *Magellan* was launched in 1989 to orbit Venus and map it using radar.

Other uses of satellites include communications (TV and telephone) and surveillance. Military surveillance satellites are used for checking on the movement of hostile warships or planes.

Many satellites are in low orbits, circling the Earth every hour or two. Others are in high orbits, staying above the same spot on Earth. These are called geostationary orbits.

▽ The Hubble Space Telescope is an orbiting observatory weighing approximately 25,000 pounds. It was placed in orbit by a space shuttle in 1990, and may be serviced and repaired by the shuttle. Compared with Earth-bound telescopes, it can reach seven times as far into space.

Into orbit

Placing commercial satellites in orbit is big business. Only a few countries have the ability to do this. Organizations in the United States, the Soviet Union, Europe and China compete for the business of launching the world's satellites.

In the United States the main means of deploying satellites is by space shuttle or Titan or other rockets. Soviet rockets include Energia and Molniya. The European rocket is Ariane 4.

▷ The European Space Agency (ESA) rocket Ariane 4 on the launch pad with the *Olympus 1* satellite below its nose cone. ESA plans a new, more powerful rocket for the mid-1990s, Ariane 5, capable of lifting 19 tons.

▽ The Soviet rocket Molniya on its way to the launch pad. It can launch payloads up to 7.5 tons.

Satellites are placed into orbit on most shuttle flights. The shuttle itself has a low orbit, at most about 560 km (347 miles) up. Satellites for higher orbits need the assistance of a rocket when released.

A new method for launching lightweight satellites into low Earth orbit is being developed in the United States. This is called Pegasus. It has wings and is launched from a high-flying aircraft. It is then blasted into orbit by a three-stage rocket.

▽ A satellite is launched spinning gently from the cargo bay of a shuttle. It has a rocket unit attached, which is fired once the satellite has moved far enough away. Such rockets are called Payload Assist Modules (PAM). They are used for sending geostationary satellites into their high orbits.

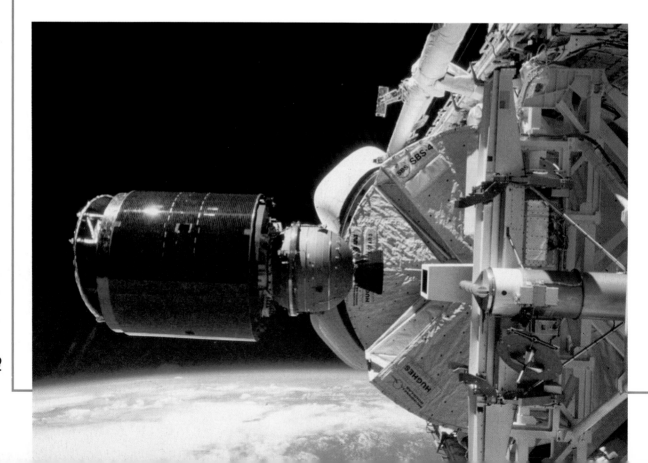

△ The Pegasus
winged satellite-
launcher attached
underneath the wing of
a modified B-52
bomber during trials.

▷ An artist's
impression of Pegasus
after being launched
from the B-52 (seen
flying off below).

Space repairs

Satellites can be retrieved in space and repaired by space shuttle astronauts. They may then be returned to orbit. Scientific experiments or damaged satellites may also be retrieved and brought back to Earth.

▷ Astronauts pose with a "For Sale" sign after rescuing two stranded satellites.

▽ An astronaut locks onto a stranded satellite to maneuver it back to the shuttle.

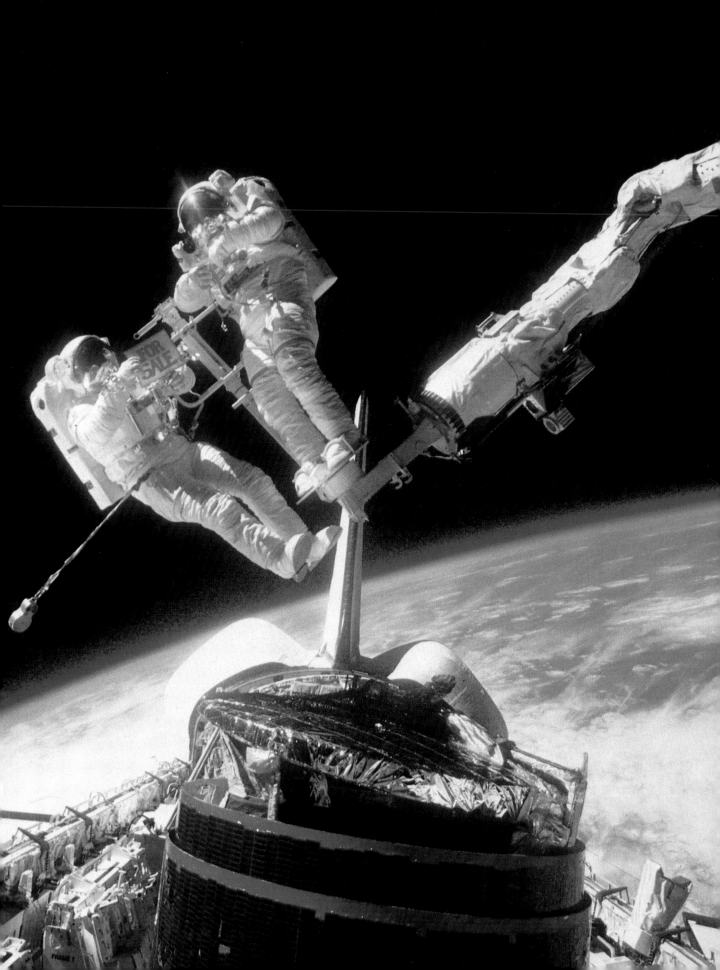

Satellites in orbit

By the start of the 1990s, there were more than 1,800 satellites circling the Earth, most of them no longer working. More than 1,000 of these were Soviet satellites, and over 500 were American. Altogether, more than 20 nations have put satellites in orbit.

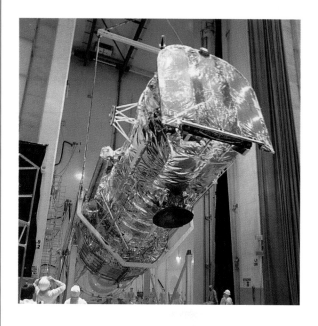

△ The Hubble Space Telescope in its foil wrapping, a protection from the Sun's heat. Weighing 25,000 pounds, it was placed into orbit by shuttle in 1990. Work had started on the project, which cost $1.5 billion, in 1978.

Space junk

In addition to satellites, there are thousands of pieces of "space junk" orbiting the Earth. Included in this debris are pieces of rocket boosters, spacecraft and worn-out satellites. Smaller bits, too small to be tracked by radar, include such items as rocket panels and camera lenses.

Counting nuts and bolts and flecks of paint, there are e billions of pieces of junk rattling around the Earth at speeds of nearly 40,000 km/h (25,000 mph).

The amount of space debris is becoming dangerous. Even a tiny particle colliding with a spacecraft at such high speeds could damage or destroy it.

High and low

Low orbits can be anything between 160 and 1,600 km (100 and 1,000 miles) high. Satellites in these orbits usually move west-east over the equator or south-north over the poles, making several orbits a day.

The so-called stationary, or geostationary, satellites orbit at a height of about 36,000 km (22,320 miles). They make one revolution of the Earth in the same time as it takes Earth to spin around once, so they stay above the same spot on Earth.

Saved by satellite

A Soviet ice station set up on a glacier in the Antarctic drifted away when a large slab of ice broke off in 1986. A radar satellite, *Cosmos 1766*, used for studying the oceans, spotted the drifting ice floe and the crew were saved.

Ship-to-shore

More than 5,000 ships at sea communicate with shore stations and other ships by satellite. These are not warships, which have their own military communications systems, but merchant ships.

The International Maritime Satellite organization has three satellites for this purpose. The service is more reliable than ship-to-shore radio, which is affected by the weather.

Space nations

By the end of the 1980s, eight nations and the European group ESA had rockets powerful enough to launch their own satellites. Their first launches were as follows:

Soviet Union	October 1957
United States	January 1958
France	November 1965
Japan	February 1970
China	April 1970
Britain	October 1971
ESA	December 1979
India	July 1980
Israel	September 1988

△ Ariane 1 blasts ESA into space in 1979.

Glossary

Geostationary orbit
A high orbit in which a satellite stays above the same spot on Earth. This is possible because it makes one complete orbit every 24 hours, the time it takes the Earth to spin around once.

Multistage rocket
A rocket built in more than one stage, usually two or three.

Orbit
The path a satellite takes around the Earth, or which any body takes around a larger body. Satellites are held in orbit by the gravity of the larger body. They travel fast enough and are far enough away not to fall toward the larger body.

PAM
Payload Assist Module – a rocket attached to a satellite to send it into a high orbit after it has been released from a space shuttle.

Payload
The cargo sent up on a rocket or in a space shuttle. Payloads include satellites, probes for studying the planets, scientific experiments and sections of space stations.

Satellite
Any body that orbits another body. The working satellites and space junk orbiting the Earth are artificial satellites, made by people on Earth. There are natural satellites, too. The Moon is a satellite of the Earth, and some planets have several moons, or natural satellites. The planets are satellites of the Sun.

Space shuttle
A reusable spacecraft.

Space station
A laboratory orbiting the Earth, with working and living quarters for scientists.

Space telescope
A telescope orbiting the Earth. The stars can be studied much better from space, where there is no atmosphere.

Stationary orbit
See Geostationary orbit.

Index

PRINTED IN BELGIUM BY
proost
INTERNATIONAL BOOK PRODUCTION